FAMILY FUNK

D0121577

FAMILY FUNK

Editing and Production Team:
Gregory C. Benoit, James F. Couch, Jr.,
Mary Chatfield, Ashley Benedict, Scott Lee

Nashville, TN

Published by Serendipity House Publishers

Nashville, Tennessee

International Standard Book Number: 1-57494-117-8

ACKNOWLEDGMENTS

Scripture quotations are taken from the
Holman Christian Standard Bible,
© Copyright 2000 by Holman Bible Publishers. Used by permission.

To Zondervan Bible Publishers for permission to use the NIV text,
The Holy Bible, New International Bible Society.
© 1973, 1978, 1984 by International Bible Society.
Used by permission of Zondervan Bible Publishers.

03 04 05 06 07 08 / 10 9 8 7 6 5 4 3 2 1

Nashville, Tennessee

1-800-525-9563

www.serendipityhouse.com

TABLE OF CONTENTS

SERENDIPITY HANG TIME

The Serendipity Hang Time Bible studies are designed for use by those who are leading small groups of young people in their study of God's Word. These books are somewhat different from other group study guides in that they actually are not group study guides; they are more of a leader's Bible study kit, a resource tool to help a Bible study leader build a seven-week Bible study custom-tailored to meet the needs of the group.

This book is intended to be a flexible study tool for youth leaders to use in helping young people deal with the realities of modern life. They are topical studies, dealing with issues such as family problems, self-esteem, existential despair, anger and aggression, sexual temptation, confusion about religion, inconsistencies in our culture, and many other struggles that are so common among teenagers.

This book is not intended to be a step-by-step study guide that a group reads through together. Rather, it is intended to be a tool for the leader to use to address pertinent questions and issues, turning to the Bible for the true answers. It provides Scripture passages to study, probing questions to ask, directions that the discussions might take, ideas for activities that make the study fun, and background information that will help make the Scriptures understandable in the 21st century.

WHAT THIS IS

Each study opens with an introduction that will offer some suggestions for what direction the discussion might take. Following this are a series of resources that a leader can use in planning out the week's study.

ACTIVITIES

This is the hands-on stuff, the opening activity that gets the group laughing together and helps them feel comfortable. There are generally two activity ideas. These ideas can also help to suggest your own ideas for activities that you create.

ICEBREAKER

This is the "icebreaker" section, the transition time from entertaining activity toward more serious discussion. It normally offers three ice-breaker questions which are very general in nature and help the group to move toward a serious consideration of God's Word.

SCRIPTURE

A Scripture passage is given, and the text is included for convenience. (Because the reading is usually broken into parts for several group members to read, you may copy the Scripture text for each member of the group.)

QUESTIONS FOR DISCUSSION

This section digs into the Bible study. The Scripture passage is followed by four to six probing questions in each of two different categories which encourage the group to look closely at what God's Word has to say on the topic of discussion. There are two types of questions here: factual, interpretive (or "head") questions which help the group to understand the passage; and practical, application (or "heart") questions that ask the group members to consider how they will put the ideas into practice in their own lives.

CARING FOR ONE ANOTHER

The "feet" of any philosophical study is the act of putting ideas into practice. In this final section the leader will find some suggestions on possible questions to ask of the group, questions that will urge each person to plan on putting into practice the ideas that have been studied. It is essential that the group spend some time in prayer during this portion of the meeting. At times suggestions will be offered to guide the prayer. Make sure you are sensitive to the concerns that the group members share during the discussions. Incorporate these concerns into the prayer time.

NEXT WEEK

Each study concludes with an overview of what will be studied in the next session. This also includes a "heads up," a note to the leader of anything that may require any advanced preparation, such as things to ask the group members to bring with them next week.

NOTES

Finally, additional notes are provided which will assist the leader in understanding such issues as the culture in which the story is taking place, background on the people in the story, and points to consider in directing the discussion.

The premise of this series is simple: use this book as a kit to use in building your own Bible study on a topic of importance to young people. Sometimes a leader has time to plan out and prepare a Bible study in advance; sometimes we all find ourselves rushing to catch up on responsibilities. This book can be used in both circumstances; a leader can simply select a few questions and activities from each section and use them in studying the passage, or he can use the materials in this book to put together his own questions, activities, and Scripture passages.

Either way, a few things are needed each week from the leader. First, read carefully through the Scripture passage that is provided, and determine what direction the discussion ought to take. Plan some sort of fun activity for an opener; it doesn't need to be complicated, but it should not be thrown together at the very last minute. Finally, and most importantly, pray! Pray that the Lord will teach you the truths from His Word, pray that you will be a good role model in practicing those truths, and pray that He will be at work in the hearts and minds of the young people in your group.

The saying, "We can choose our friends but we can't choose our families," is true both literally and suggestively—it suggests the problems that our family members can make in our lives, and hints that for many of us we'd choose differently if someone had asked our opinion.

Families, of course, are nothing new—they've been around since the very beginning in the Garden of Eden. The very first human beings formed a family of their own, became dysfunctional, and the trouble has continued ever since. We speak casually these days about dysfunctional families, but one would certainly describe a family in those terms if the eldest son murdered his younger brother. Cain murdered Abel because Abel's sacrifice to God was received with pleasure and his wasn't. Perhaps these two brothers symbolize much of what can go wrong, not just within families, but between all people in general.

The truth is that all humans are broken by sin, and therefore all humans will sin against other humans. It sounds simplistic in a way, but it is a vital truth which we must remember when we begin discussing family life. All families are composed of broken people who sin, so all families will experience sinful behavior. This truth is at the heart of this study on family life. It is no accident that this book is entitled Family Funk; if family life were always fun and laughter then there would be no need for this Bible study.

Unfortunately, families in our day are under severe attack from society as a whole and from Satan in particular. Young people find themselves dealing with alcoholic or drug-addicted parents, hateful and murderous siblings, broken homes, family units that are a forced amalgam of numerous previous marriages, sexual and physical abuse from family members, and many other horrible trials that should never be inflicted on anyone.

Fortunately—and this is the irony—these problems are not new! It is fortunate because families since the beginning of history have dealt with such sins as these, and the Word of God records the lives and experiences of many who made this joyful discovery: God is in control even when we are not.

This study is designed to bring out that very truth: God is in control. We will look at the stories of many different families in the coming weeks, families that experienced "blended homes," physical abuse, hatred, envy, parents who couldn't get along, and even an orphan. In the process of these studies, we will allow our group members to discover first that they are not alone in the pains and struggles of their families, and second that God has worked through—many times before—such people as themselves, and He can do it again today.

HANG TIME

FAMILY FUNK

MARReGE

MARRIAGE

GENESIS 1:26-28; 2:15-25; EPHESIANS 5:22-33

The basis of any true family is founded on marriage, so this seems like a good place to begin in our study. This topic will actually be in two parts, with "Divorce" forming the second study. Scripture has much to say about marriage, and a group could easily spend the entire seven weeks on the topic. It might be helpful, however, to begin our study of the family by learning just what marriage is: the indissoluble union of two people becoming one flesh. We will begin at the beginning, in the Garden of Eden, getting to know the very first married couple, Adam and Eve. When God created people He invented marriage.

This will be a good chance for some members of your group to learn just what marriage is all about, and to begin planning ahead for the day when they will choose a mate for themselves. Some of this topic may prove a bit controversial, as it touches upon the concept of roles within marriage. Paul teaches in Ephesians that husbands and wives have different roles to play, and he points out that only when both parties are properly doing their jobs will the marriage reflect the image of God. It may be helpful to approach this with an understanding of the concept of "submission," since this may be the point where our culture takes issue with what Scripture says.

Jesus commands all believers to submit to one another, just as He submits to the Father. He even washed His own disciples' feet, then commanded them to do so for others. This is the attitude involved in submission: to voluntarily give up one's rights and expectations in order to serve someone else. It is not that the person who submits is inferior; on the contrary, it is that the person submitting has chosen to serve others, regardless of whether one is somehow superior or not.

Christ modeled this servant love that has become the standard which husbands are to use in loving their wives, and this command must not be overlooked. It is a very high calling, for it means voluntarily protecting and serving another, even if that other person is uncaring or ungrateful. Both parties—husbands and wives—are called to serve one another and not themselves, and this is the basic point of our first lesson.

ACTIVITIES

CHOOSE ONE OF THE ACTIVITIES BELOW

Know Your Partner
Pair off everyone in the group; if there is an odd number, the leader sits out. Take two minutes for one person in each couple to tell the other about him or herself, then have them switch from telling to listening. At the end of the time bring the group back together and have each person introduce his or her partner to the group.

Noah's Ark
Write down the names of animals on little slips of paper, one animal per slip. Make certain that you have two slips with the same animal—two elephant slips, etc.—and make certain that you have the

same number of slips as you have group members. The goal here is to have everyone find a mate, so there must be a mate for every slip handed out. Each person draws a slip, then puts on a blindfold. When all group members are blindfolded, they must walk around making noises imitating their animal. The object is to find the other person who is the same animal.

ICEBREAKERS

CHOOSE ONE OR TWO OF THESE ICEBREAKERS

○ How did your parents meet?

○ If you could marry any famous person in the world (regardless of when he or she lived), who would it be and why?

○ If you were getting married, and money were no object, where would you have the wedding? The honeymoon?

SCRIPTURE READING

READ THE FOLLOWING PASSAGES

Have the group read the following passages from Genesis and Ephesians. Assign students who feel comfortable reading aloud the different roles. If you don't have enough for all of the roles, either have some read more than one part or read some of the portions yourself.

Genesis 1

Reader One: [26] Then God said, "Let us make man in our image, in our likeness, and let them rule over the fish of the sea and the birds of the air, over the livestock, over all the earth, and over all the creatures that move along the ground." [27] So God created man in his own image, in the image of God he created him; male and female he created them.

Reader Two: [28] God blessed them and said to them, "Be fruitful and increase in number; fill the earth and subdue it. Rule over the fish of the sea and the birds of the air and over every living creature that moves on the ground."

Genesis 2

Reader Three: [15] The LORD God took the man and put him in the Garden of Eden to work it and take care of it. [16] And the LORD God commanded the man, "You are free to eat from any tree in the garden; [17] but you must not eat from the tree of the knowledge of good and evil, for when you eat of it you will surely die." [18] The LORD God said, "It is not good for the man to be alone. I will make a helper suitable for him."

Reader Four: [19] Now the LORD God had formed out of the ground all the beasts of the field and all the birds of the air. He brought them to the man to see what he would name them; and whatever the man called each living creature, that was its name. [20] So the man gave names to all the livestock, the birds of the air and all the beasts of the field. But for Adam no suitable helper was found. [21] So the LORD God caused the man to fall into a deep sleep; and while he was sleeping, he took one of the man's ribs and closed up the place with flesh. ²² Then the LORD God made a woman from the rib he had taken out of the man, and he brought her to the man.

Reader One: ²³ The man said, "This is now bone of my bones and flesh of my flesh; she shall be called 'woman,' for she was taken out of man." ²⁴ For this reason a man will leave his father and mother and be united to his wife, and they will become one flesh. ²⁵ The man and his wife were both naked, and they felt no shame.

Ephesians 5
Reader Two: ²² Wives, submit   to your own husbands as to the Lord, ²³ for the husband is head of the wife as also Christ is head of the church. He is the Savior of the body. ²⁴ Now as the church submits to Christ, so wives should submit to their husbands in everything. ²⁵ Husbands, love your wives, just as also Christ loved the church and gave Himself for her, ²⁶ to make her holy, cleansing her in the washing of water by the word. ²⁷ He did this to present the church to Himself in splendor, without spot or wrinkle or any such thing, but holy and blameless. ²⁸ In the same way, husbands should love their wives as their own bodies. He who loves his wife loves himself. ²⁹ For no one ever hates his own flesh, but provides and cares for it, just as Christ does for the church, ³⁰ since we are members of His body.

Reader Three: ³¹ For this reason a man will leave his father and mother and be joined to his wife, and the two will become one flesh. ³² This mystery is profound, but I am talking about Christ and the church. ³³ To sum up, each one of you is to love his wife as himself, and the wife is to respect her husband.

Genesis 1:26–28; 2:15–25 (NIV); Ephesians 5:22–33

DISCUSSION QUESTIONS

SELECT FOUR OR FIVE QUESTIONS FROM THE HEAD AND/OR HEART SECTIONS, AND/OR MAKE UP YOUR OWN

○ Why was "no suitable helper" (Gen. 2:20) found for Adam? What exactly is a "suitable helper"?

○ Why is it "not good for man to be alone" (Gen. 2:18)? What is God's intention in creating a mate for him?

○ What does it mean to "become one flesh" (Gen. 2:24)?

○ If the entire church is called to live humbly together (1 Pet. 5:5-7), why are wives reminded to submit to their husbands (Eph. 5:22)? What does this submission mean?

○ In what way did Christ love the church? What does this mean for husbands, if they are commanded to do the same for their wives?

○ What does it mean for a man to love his wife as he loves himself (Eph. 5:33)? Give some practical examples.

○ If you could design your own perfect mate, what would you want?

○ Why do you think that God created two sexes in the first place?

○ In what ways does marriage enrich the life of a man or a woman? In what ways does it complicate it?

○ How does it make you feel to hear Paul command wives to submit to their husbands? What sort of person would you want to marry if you were going to be submitting to him?

○ What should a husband do when his own needs or desires are not the same as his wife's? According to Paul, should he demand that she submit, or sacrifice his own interests for hers?

CARING FOR ONE ANOTHER

USE THESE QUESTIONS OR MAKE UP YOUR OWN

○ Do you trust God to lead you to the right mate? If He did if for Adam and Eve, will He do it for you?

○ Are you willing to wait until you are married to have sex?

○ Spend time in prayer for your parents, asking God to bless and strengthen their marriage.

○ Spend time praying for God to lead you to the right mate, and that He will teach you beforehand how to be a good mate.

This week we considered what God intended marriage to be, and looked at the first married couple in history. In the coming week, spend time in prayer for married people you know, and also ask God to prepare you to be a good husband or wife. Next week we will consider the sad reality of what happens when a marriage ends in divorce.

NOTES

NOTES ON GENESIS 1:26-28; 2:15-25; EPHESIANS 5:22-33

Genesis

1:27 God created man in his own image. Being made in God's image means that mankind is different from the rest of creation. This difference includes man's free will— the capability to choose between right and wrong. Man quickly chose evil over good by eating the forbidden fruit (Gen. 3), and one of the things that suffered was the marriage of Adam and Eve (Gen. 3:7). Today, thousands of years later, sin still causes destruction within marriages, resulting in (and often caused by) high rates of divorce and couples living together outside of marriage. While this study does not delve into man's original sin, it is important to recognize that it is at the root of marital breakdown. **male and female he created them.** Scripture elsewhere gives direction on roles within marriage, but right from the beginning God ordained that men and women both shared the image of God. God chose to create two sexes so that together they could form a more complete picture of His divine nature, each sex offering an emphasis on specific attributes of God.

2:16 You are free. God gave us free will, the freedom to choose. One aspect of free will is both a blessing—giving us the freedom to choose whom or whether to marry—and a responsibility—requiring that we continually choose to be faithful to God and to our mate. Paul emphasizes this responsibility in his teachings on marriage.

2:18 It is not good. This is true in a couple of ways. Practically, Adam needed Eve if the race was to grow. Socially, Adam needed help, as is illustrated by God's next words. **a helper.** God seems to intend marriage to be a partnership, two people working together on the same project (dominion of the earth, v. 15), each of whom offers unique gifts which are necessary to success. This unified team was fractured as soon as the forbidden fruit was eaten. First, both were ashamed and tried to hide their nakedness. Then they tried to hide from God, and finally Adam turned on Eve by blaming her for his own sin. Paul reiterates the importance of mutual respect and teamwork in 1 Corinthians 7.

2:24 one flesh. God's original plan for marriage was that the couple would be united as one flesh. This meant that divorce would have been as unthinkable as cutting off one's limbs, and sex would have only been shared within that sacred union.

Ephesians

5:22 submit to your own husbands. The concept of a woman submitting to a man is very controversial in our culture; we tend to fixate on individual rights and freedoms. It is significant that Paul does not focus on rights or freedoms in this passage, but rather on responsibilities and roles. A woman has the right to do what she desires, but the godly wife will choose to submit to her husband just the same. This directive is given in the context of the entire body of Christ living in submission to its head, Christ.

5:25 as also Christ loved the church. Jesus demonstrated his love for the church by dying for her, even while she was in sinful rebellion against him (Rom. 5:8). This is a very weighty responsibility, and a young man should know in advance that he will be called upon to put his wife's good before his own, even to the point of sacrifice regardless of how much she merits it.

HANG TIME

FAMILY FUNK

Last week we considered the ideal marriage, learning about what God originally intended it to be. Real life, however, is not always ideal, and today approximately half of all marriages in the United States end in divorce. It is important that we remember God's original plan for what marriage should look like as we consider what the Scriptures have to say about divorce. It will help us to understand why God says that He hates divorce if we remember the tremendous gift that marriage was intended to be. Also it will help us to see that God is a giver of good gifts, not an angry slave-driver who insists that we remain miserable.

There will likely be members of your group whose parents have been divorced or are now going through a divorce. The goal of the study is not to condemn the parents, but rather to present the students with God's truth and to encourage them to make it their goal.

Rather than study the biographies of people from the Bible, this week we will focus on what Jesus Himself had to say about divorce, and then listen as Paul takes the Lord's teachings and applies them to real-life situations. The reason for this is that every couple's situation is unique, and many married people feel that their lives are intolerable in their present marriage. Jesus asks us to simply obey His words, regardless of our circumstances, and Paul spells out clearly just what the obedience will mean.

Some of our studies in this book will be hard for members of your group, because they will find that the topic hits close to home. This is one of those hard topics. It may bring out discussion that is emotionally charged because the teachings are difficult to accept in today's culture. Yet if we are to follow the teachings of Jesus, we must often wrestle with some teachings that are costly. The real goal in this study, then, is not to condemn or to find fault with others who have been divorced, but rather to train the next generation in how to build solid, lasting marriages.

ACTIVITIES

CHOOSE ONE OF THE ACTIVITIES BELOW

O **Overcoming Obstacles**
Have the group stand to begin an imaginary pantomime journey. The leader will describe the journey—"We begin by walking through a field"—and each person will act out (in place or moving around) the situation by pretending to be walking through high grass, and so forth. Include a variety of obstacles, such as crossing a deep stream, climbing a cliff, leaping over ditches, crossing busy streets, etc.

O **Picking Favorites**
Divide the group into pairs, then have them describe their favorite flavor of ice cream with one another. If they both have the same favorite, they remain together for the next round; otherwise, during round two, they must find someone whose favorite flavor is different from their previous partner's. Next, have the new partners tell each other what their favorite color is, and repeat the process. After four or five switches, the people with the fewest switches win a prize.

ICEBREAKERS

CHOOSE ONE OR TWO OF THESE ICEBREAKERS

○ What certificates or awards have you received? Which one means the most to you?

○ In what circumstances are you most likely to become stubborn? When are you most flexible?

○ Have you ever "renounced" a habit? What was the habit, and how did you break it?

SCRIPTURE READING

READ THE FOLLOWING PASSAGES

Matthew 19

Reader One: ³ Some Pharisees approached Him to test Him. They asked, "Is it lawful for a man to divorce his wife on any grounds?"

⁴ "Haven't you read," He replied, "that He who created them in the beginning made them male and female, ⁵ and He also said:

> For this reason a man will leave his father and mother and be joined to his wife, and the two will become one flesh?

⁶ So they are no longer two, but one flesh. Therefore what God has joined together, man must not separate."

Reader Two: ⁷ "Why then," they asked Him, "did Moses command us to give divorce papers and to send her away?"

⁸ He told them, "Moses permitted you to divorce your wives because of the hardness of your hearts. But it was not like that from the beginning. ⁹ And I tell you, whoever divorces his wife, except for sexual immorality, and marries another, commits adultery."

Reader Three: ¹⁰ His disciples said to Him, "If the relationship of a man with his wife is like this, it's better not to marry!"

¹¹ But He told them, "Not everyone can accept this saying, but only those to whom it has been given. ¹² For there are eunuchs who were born that way from their mother's womb, there are eunuchs who were made by men, and there are eunuchs who have made themselves that way because of the kingdom of heaven. Let anyone accept this who can."

1 Corinthians 7

Reader Four: ¹⁰ I command the married—not I, but the Lord—a wife is not to leave her husband. ¹¹ But if she does leave, she must remain unmarried or be reconciled to her husband—and a husband is not to leave his wife. ¹² But to the rest I, not the Lord, say: If any brother has an unbelieving wife, and she is willing to live with him, he must not leave her. ¹³ Also, if any woman has an unbelieving husband, and he is willing to live with her, she must not leave her husband. ¹⁴ For the unbelieving husband is sanctified by the wife, and the unbelieving wife is sanctified by the Christian husband. Otherwise your children would be unclean, but now they are holy. [15] But if the unbeliever leaves, let him leave. A brother or a sister is not bound in such cases. God has called you to peace. [16] For you, wife, how do you know whether you will save your husband? Or you, husband, how do you know whether you will save your wife?

Reader Five: [28] However, if you do get married, you have not sinned, and if a virgin marries, she has not sinned. But such people will have trouble in this life, and I am trying to spare you. ...
[32] I want you to be without concerns. An unmarried man is concerned about the things of the Lord—how he may please the Lord. [33] But a married man is concerned about the things of the world—how he may please his wife— [34] and he is divided. An unmarried woman or a virgin is concerned about the things of the Lord, so that she may be holy both in body and in spirit. But a married woman is concerned about the things of the world—how she may please her husband. [35] Now I am saying this for your own benefit, not to put a restraint on you, but because of what is proper, and so that you may be devoted to the Lord without distraction. ...
[39] A wife is bound as long as her husband is living. But if her husband dies, she is free to be married to anyone she wants—only in the Lord. [40] But she is happier if she remains as she is, in my opinion. And I think that I also have the Spirit of God.

Matthew 19:3–12; 1 Corinthians 7:10–16,28,32–35,39–40

DISCUSSION QUESTIONS

SELECT FOUR OR FIVE QUESTIONS FROM THE HEAD AND/OR
HEART SECTIONS, AND/OR MAKE UP YOUR OWN

○ Why does Jesus emphasize that a married couple are "one flesh" (Matt. 19:5)? What does this mean?

○ If married people are like one body, what is divorce like?

○ What is "marital unfaithfulness" (Matt. 19:9)?

○ What are legitimate reasons for ending a marriage? (Consider both passages, from Matt. and 1 Cor.)

○ What are some reasons that a person might decide to remain single?

○ Christians are commanded not to marry non-Christians (2 Cor. 6:14–16). Why, then, does Paul give instructions for those married to unbelievers (1 Cor. 7:12–16)?

○ How has divorce affected you or someone you know?

○ What reasons do people use nowadays when deciding to divorce? How do these reasons match up with the teachings of Scripture?

○ What things in the world today tempt people to

be unfaithful to their spouses? What affect does unfaithfulness have on their marriages?

○ How does a person know if he or she is being called by God to remain single?

○ What are the costs of singleness? The benefits?

○ Why it is important to have an understanding about what is a legitimate reason for divorce before marrying someone?

○ Why is it important for Christians not to marry non-Christians?

 ## CARING FOR ONE ANOTHER

USE THESE QUESTIONS OR MAKE UP YOUR OWN

○ If you are suffering from a divorce, how can the group help and support you?

○ How will you plan now to marry only a Christian?

○ How will you prepare yourself now to avoid divorce when you are older?

○ Do you think that the Lord might want you to remain single? Why? If so, how will this affect your life this week?

This week we wrestled with the Lord's high standards concerning divorce. In the coming week, spend time in prayer for those who are married, asking God to strengthen their resolve to remain together. Next week we will consider the tensions that often exist among brothers and sisters, which we call sibling rivalry. [Optional: Next week, bring a white t-shirt or some other old shirt for tie-dying. We will be making our own colorful clothes!]

NOTES ON MATTHEW 19:3-12;
1 CORINTHIANS 7:10-16,28,32-35,39-40

Matthew

19:5 one flesh. Jesus reminds His listeners of God's original plan for marriage, made clear at creation: that two people should become as solidly bound together as the parts of a person's body. Understanding the Lord's clear teachings on divorce, as well as those of Paul, requires that we begin with a clear recognition of the solemnity of marriage.

19:6 man must not separate. Paul underscores Jesus' teaching here, stating in 1 Corinthians 7:39 that death (God's action) is a legitimate end to a marriage, but divorce (man's action is a very serious thing).

19:12 eunuchs. Jesus seems to be using the term eunuch—a castrated male—in a symbolic sense to mean a person who does not have a strong desire or need for marital intimacy. In this sense, some are born that way, simply feeling no strong desire to get married; others have found themselves in circumstances or conditions which make marriage impossible (such as physical handicaps, emotional issues, war, or any of countless circumstances); still others have chosen deliberately to remain unmarried in order to devote themselves to God's work of service to others.

1 Corinthians
7:10 not I, but the Lord. In verse 12, Paul reverses this phrase in order to distinguish between godly advice and direction from the Lord. Some feel that the first command, "a wife must not separate from her husband" (v. 10), can be directly tied to the Lord's clear teachings in Matthew, while the special situations of an unequally yoked couple (v. 12f) is Paul's application of this command to real-life situations. Regardless, the biblical model is the same: Christians are ideally not to divorce their spouses for any reason except adultery. (Paul's focus on the wife does not mean that these principles do not apply to Christian husbands.)

7:12 an unbelieving wife. This is not an endorsement of unequally yoked marriages, granting permission to a Christian to marry a non-Christian, but rather Paul's recognition of real-life circumstances. Some Christians married non-Christians but they are not free to later change their minds and divorce. Others may have come to Christ later in life, but had a spouse who remained an unbeliever. In all these cases, the Christian is not to initiate divorce.

7:35 devoted to the Lord without distraction. Paul is not making a case here for any moral or spiritual superiority of celibacy over marriage. Rather, he is urging all believers, whether married or single, to strive to be fully devoted to God and to serving others. He does point out, however, that for many it is easier to do this without the commitments of marriage (v. 40).

HANG TIME

FAMILY FUNK

3 SIBLING RIVALRY: THE PROBLEM

GENESIS 37:2-12,14-18,21-28,31-36

Sibling rivalry is a term that can refer to something as subtle as trying to "fill the shoes" of an older brother or sister, hoping to live up to a brother's or sister's accomplishments. However, it can be far more serious than that at times, even to the point of a deep-seated hatred. Consider, for example, the tragic example of Cain and Abel (Gen. 4).

In this week's study we will be looking at a case of such extreme sibling rivalry, between Joseph and his ten brothers. Joseph's father is Jacob, renamed Israel, a man who understood very well the dangers of a parent choosing favorites. Jacob was a "mama's boy" (Rebekah's favorite), but his twin brother, Esau, was "daddy's pal" (Isaac's favorite). This favoritism encouraged a dangerous rivalry between Jacob and Esau, which resulted in Jacob's treacherous swindling of Esau and Esau's ensuing resentment. (See Genesis 25 and following for the entire story.)

Unfortunately, as so often happens, Jacob did not learn to avoid his parents' mistakes, but he repeated them himself when he had a family of his own. In this chapter we will discover that Jacob (Israel) loved his son Joseph more than any of his other sons, a favoritism which was painfully obvious to the whole family. The reason for this is that Jacob had two wives and two concubines, each of whom bore sons, but he loved his wife Rachel the most. Rachel bore two sons to Jacob— Joseph and Benjamin—and he loved them more than his ten other sons.

There are numerous other examples in Scripture of dangerous sibling rivalries. Certainly the hatred and resentment which Cain bore against his brother, Abel, is a prime example. We will focus on Joseph and his brothers, however, because it is a two-part story, one with a very happy ending. Next week we will consider the second half, in which Joseph is fully reconciled with his brothers.

This week we will examine sibling rivalry in its ugliest form, and consider our own family stories in terms of getting along with brothers and sisters. Joseph provides an example of how to do it right (as opposed to Cain, who did it very wrong), and in the end he breaks the cycle of parental favoritism which is so often at the root of such hatred.

Another facet of this story is that Joseph grew up in a "blended family," where he and his brothers had the same father but different mothers. This is relevant today, and there may well be members of your own group who have non-traditional family situations. This will be an important issue to touch on if that is the case, since such blended homes can often bring difficult interactions among the various children. In such situations, favoritism may be an issue that some in your group are struggling with, and it will be a real encouragement to discover that some of the great "heroes of the faith" also struggled with the same problems.

This week, encourage the group to consider their own relationships with brothers and sisters, and allow them to be confronted with the dangers of resentment, favoritism, and hatred.

ACTIVITIES

CHOOSE ONE OF THE ACTIVITIES BELOW

○ **Create a Shirt of Many Colors**
Have group members bring a white T-shirt to study this week. [NOTE: THIS WAS MENTIONED IN THE PREVIOUS STUDY.] Prepare clothes dyes of different colors, and have a tie-dying party.

○ **Create a Dream**
Begin the story by saying, "Last night I dreamed that I was...." The next person then continues the story with a short phrase or sentence, invented on the spot. Continue around the group and allow each person to continue the dream story and see just how bizarre your dream was!

ICEBREAKERS

CHOOSE ONE OR TWO OF THESE ICEBREAKERS

○ If you could have a custom-designed coat, with no limit to cost, what would it be like?

○ If you could choose one rock star for a brother or sister, who would it be?

○ What is the most exotic animal you've ever seen?

SCRIPTURE READING

READ THE FOLLOWING PASSAGES

Reader One: ² This is the account of Jacob. Joseph, a young man of seventeen, was tending the flocks with his brothers, the sons of Bilhah and the sons of Zilpah, his father's wives, and he brought their father a bad report about them.

³ Now Israel loved Joseph more than any of his other sons, because he had been born to him in his old age; and he made a richly ornamented robe for him. ⁴ When his brothers saw that their father loved him more than any of them, they hated him and could not speak a kind word to him.

Reader Two: ⁵ Joseph had a dream, and when he told it to his brothers, they hated him all the more. ⁶ He said to them, "Listen to this dream I had: ⁷ We were binding sheaves of grain out in the field when suddenly my sheaf rose and stood upright, while your sheaves gathered around mine and bowed down to it."

⁸ His brothers said to him, "Do you intend to reign over us? Will you actually rule us?" And they hated him all the more because of his dream and what he had said.

⁹ Then he had another dream, and he told it to his brothers. "Listen," he said, "I had another dream, and this time the sun and moon and eleven stars were bowing down to me."

¹⁰ When he told his father as well as his brothers, his father rebuked him and said, "What is this dream you had? Will your mother

and I and your brothers actually come and bow down to the ground before you?" ¹¹ His brothers were jealous of him, but his father kept the matter in mind.

Reader Three: ¹² Now his brothers had gone to graze their father's flocks near Shechem, Israel said to Joseph, "As you know, your brothers are grazing the flocks near Shechem. Come, I am going to send you to them." "Very well," he replied.
¹⁴ So he said to him, "Go and see if all is well with your brothers and with the flocks, and bring word back to me." Then he sent him off from the Valley of Hebron. ¹⁷ ...So Joseph went after his brothers and found them near Dothan. ¹⁸ But they saw him in the distance, and before he reached them, they plotted to kill him....

Reader Four: ²¹ When Reuben heard this, he tried to rescue him from their hands. "Let's not take his life," he said. ²² "Don't shed any blood. Throw him into this cistern here in the desert, but don't lay a hand on him." Reuben said this to rescue him from them and take him back to his father.
²³ So when Joseph came to his brothers, they stripped him of his robe—the richly ornamented robe he was wearing— ²⁴ and they took him and threw him into the cistern. Now the cistern was empty; there was no water in it.

Reader Five: ²⁵ As they sat down to eat their meal, they looked up and saw a caravan of Ishmaelites coming from Gilead. ²⁶ Judah said to his brothers, "What will we gain if we kill our brother and cover up his blood? ²⁷ Come, let's sell him to the Ishmaelites...."

²⁸ So when the Midianite merchants came by, his brothers pulled Joseph up out of the cistern and sold him for twenty shekels of silver to the Ishmaelites, who took him to Egypt. ...

³¹ Then they got Joseph's robe, slaughtered a goat and dipped the robe in the blood. ³² They took the ornamented robe back to their father and said, "We found this. Examine it to see whether it is your son's robe." ...

³⁶ Meanwhile, the Midianites sold Joseph in Egypt to Potiphar, one of Pharaoh's officials, the captain of the guard.

Genesis 37:2-12,14-18,21-28,31-36 (NIV)

DISCUSSION QUESTIONS

SELECT FOUR OR FIVE QUESTIONS FROM THE HEAD OR HEART SECTIONS, AND/OR MAKE UP YOUR OWN

○ Israel (Jacob) "loved Joseph more than any of his other sons" (v. 3). Why was Joseph his favorite? What affect did the favoritism have on the family?

○ Why do Joseph's brothers hate him? What things does Joseph do that increase their resentment? What things does Jacob do?

○ Who was most at fault for all this family tension? Who was least: Joseph, Israel, the brothers?

○ After throwing Joseph into the cistern (see

Notes), his brothers sat down to eat lunch. What does this reveal about their feelings for him? Do they seem sorry for their sin?

○ What is Judah's motive in persuading his brothers not to kill Joseph (v. 26)? How does this compare with Rueben's motives (v. 21, 22)?

○ If you have brothers or sisters, how well do you all get along? Is there any rivalry between you?

○ Do your parents pick favorites? If so, what affect does it have on your relationships with brothers and sisters? If not, how do your parents communicate their love equally?

○ If you are in a "blended family," how well do you get along with your half-brothers and sisters? Do your parents communicate their love equally?

○ How do you think Joseph's brothers should have addressed their father's favoritism? How do you address parental favoritism in your own family? How should you?

○ Do you ever feel hatred for your brothers or sisters? If so, how do you deal with that hatred? What should Joseph's brothers have done about their resentments toward Joseph?

CARING FOR ONE ANOTHER

USE THESE QUESTIONS OR MAKE UP YOUR OWN

○ How can the group pray for you in your relationships with your siblings? With your parents?

○ How can you become a better brother or sister in your own family? A better parent?

○ What will you do in the coming week to overcome resentment or anger toward your family?

NEXT WEEK

This week we learned about the terrible tensions that existed within one family, a deadly rivalry between Joseph and his brothers. In the coming week, pray for your own brothers and sisters, asking that God would bless them and make them like His Son. Next week we will learn more about this family, and discover that they had a very happy ending. [Optional: Also, please bring in one picture of yourself from when you were a baby, or as a kid in a funny situation. We will use them in our opening games.]

NOTES ON GENESIS 37:2-12,14-18,21-28,31-36

37:2 sons of Bilhah and the sons of Zilpah. Israel had two wives—Rachel and Leah—and two concubines (Gen. 35). These are all actually Joseph's half brothers; it is what we today would call a blended family—with four different mothers. **he brought their father a bad report about them.** We don't know what this bad report was; perhaps Joseph reported to his father on the brothers' behavior while out keeping sheep, which might also explain Jacob's decision to send Joseph out to his brothers in the field. (The following chapter, concerning Judah and Tamar, demonstrates that the brothers' behavior was not always exemplary.) Regardless, even if Joseph had been a "tattle-tale" against his brothers, it does not justify a hatred that amounts to attempted murder.

37:3 Israel loved Joseph more than any of his other sons. Jacob, referred to in this passage by his new name of Israel, grew up with parental favoritism (Gen. 25:28) and had seen first-hand its devastating effects on a family. He ought to have known better, yet this shows the common danger of carrying on dysfunctional patterns in subsequent generations (Ex. 20:5). **richly ornamented robe.** This was probably a very costly garment, perhaps even somewhat ostentatious, which would have been suitable for a prince (2 Sam. 13:18).

37:5–9 Joseph's dreams both prophesy that his entire family would one day bow before him. (Next week we shall see the fulfillment of the dreams.) Given the preferential treatment Joseph was already receiving, it is easy to understand why his brothers would be offended by the dreams. What is important to note, however, is that the dreams do come true despite the murderous hatred and deliberate sabotage of his brothers. Our very own family may turn against us, yet God's plan for our lives cannot be thwarted.

37:10 What is this dream you had? The family's indignation is almost humorous, as though Joseph had deliberately chosen to have the dream. The real problem at the heart of these family disputes is jealousy and a rejection of God's plans.

37:22 cistern. Cisterns were pits used for collecting and storing water in the dry climate of the middle east. They were usually deep pits with a very narrow mouth, covered often with a large stone. Even when they were empty, the bottom was usually very muddy, sometimes deep enough that a person thrown in would be in danger of drowning just from the deep mud. Jeremiah was also thrown into an empty cistern, used as a sort of prison cell (Jer. 38:6).

37:25 they sat down to eat their meal. Joseph's brothers are so callous, so hardened in their hatred of him, that they can calmly sit next to the cistern and eat lunch as though they'd done nothing unusual.

37:26 let's sell him to the Ishmaelites. Judah persuades his brothers not to murder Joseph, not out of any sense of repentance, but rather out of greed—murder brings no profit, but slavery does. Yet note his hypocritical justification in verse 27. Reuben appears to be the only one of the ten (Benjamin is not among them) with any sense of concern for his brother. Interestingly, Jesus comes through the line of Judah, not Reuben (Matt. 1:1–6), suggesting that God can redeem and use even the most hardened sinner.

FAMILY FUNK

SIBLING RIVALRY: THE SOLUTION

GENESIS 41:56—42:24; 45:1-8; 50:15-21

Last week, we considered the problems inherent in both sibling rivalry and parental favoritism. This week we will continue our study of Joseph and his brothers, focusing on the importance of forgiveness and reconciliation.

There are actually two major lessons in this study: to be like Joseph and forgive those who have injured us, and to be like Joseph's brothers and repent of the injuries which we have done to others. Both of these elements must be present to some degree in bringing about reconciliation between family members.

In these chapters, Joseph tests his brothers to discover whether they have truly repented of their terrible sins against him. His goal is not to play God, to try and read their hearts to determine whether or not their repentance is sincere. Rather, he is just looking for evidence of it, and since he has not seen his brothers in many years he has no other way to find out.

Judah speaks on behalf of the ten for the most part in this section, and his words and actions indicate a very real repentance. In fact, he has changed so dramatically that he is willing to sacrifice his own life in exchange for Benjamin. His example is important, because we all will be guilty of mistreating family members at some point, and the Lord desires that we learn to sacrifice our own desires and goals in order to serve others. Judah has finally learned that lesson, and this allows him to be reconciled with Joseph and with his father.

Members of your group may well be struggling with these problems at home, perhaps in the role of bully, perhaps that of victim, or even both at the same time. Some may be only children or have non-traditional homes. Be careful to include them in the discussion. Take time to read the entire story of Joseph's reconciliation, found in Genesis 42—50.

ACTIVITIES

CHOOSE ONE OF THE ACTIVITIES BELOW

○ **Name that Face**
Have your group members bring in baby pictures or funny photos of themselves as little children. Show them one at a time to the group, and have the group guess who is in each photo.

○ **Joseph and His Brothers**
This game is like the old favorite "fruits and vegetables." Have the group sit in a circle, with one person in the middle standing up. Each person in the circle selects the name of one of Joseph's brothers (found in Gen. 35:23-26), and the person in the center is "Joseph." "Joseph" has a rolled up newspaper in hand, and begins the game by saying, "Joseph calls Judah." The person who is "Judah" must quickly say "Judah calls [another name]" before getting hit with the newspaper. The object is for "Joseph" to tap someone with the newspaper before that person can call on someone else. If so, the two switch places and start over.

ICEBREAKERS

CHOOSE ONE OR TWO OF THESE ICEBREAKERS

○ Have you ever been in a situation where you didn't recognize someone that you know well? Why did you not recognize that person? How did you finally realize who it was?

○ What was the best surprise gift you've ever received? What's the best one you've ever given?

○ Who is the most frightening authority figure (teacher, principal, bus driver, etc.) in your school?

SCRIPTURE READING

READ THE FOLLOWING PASSAGES

Genesis 41

Reader One: ⁵⁶ When the famine had spread over the whole country, Joseph opened the storehouses and sold grain to the Egyptians, for the famine was severe throughout Egypt. ⁵⁷ And all the countries came to Egypt to buy grain from Joseph, because the famine was severe in all the world.

Genesis 42

Reader Two: ¹ When Jacob learned that there was grain in Egypt, he said to his sons, "Why do you just keep looking at each other?" ² He continued, "I have heard that there is grain in Egypt. Go down there and buy some for us, so that we may live and not die."

³ Then ten of Joseph's brothers went down to buy grain from Egypt. ⁴ But Jacob did not send Benjamin, Joseph's brother, with the others, because he was afraid that harm might come to him. ⁵ So Israel's sons were among those who went to buy grain, for the famine was in the land of Canaan also.

⁶ Now Joseph was the governor of the land, the

one who sold grain to all its people. So when Joseph's brothers arrived, they bowed down to him with their faces to the ground. [7] As soon as Joseph saw his brothers, he recognized them, but he pretended to be a stranger and spoke harshly to them. "Where do you come from?" he asked. "From the land of Canaan," they replied, "to buy food."

Reader Three: [8] Although Joseph recognized his brothers, they did not recognize him. [9] Then he remembered his dreams about them and said to them, "You are spies! You have come to see where our land is unprotected."

[10] "No, my lord," they answered. "Your servants have come to buy food. [11] We are all the sons of one man. Your servants are honest men, not spies."

[12] "No!" he said to them. "You have come to see where our land is unprotected." [13] But they replied, "Your servants were twelve brothers, the sons of one man, who lives in the land of Canaan. The youngest is now with our father, and one is no more."

[14] Joseph said to them, "It is just as I told you: You are spies! [15] And this is how you will be tested: As surely as Pharaoh lives, you will not leave this place unless your youngest brother comes here. [16] Send one of your number to get your brother; the rest of you will be kept in prison, so that your words may be tested to see if you are telling the truth. If you are not, then as surely as Pharaoh lives, you are spies!" [17] And he put them all in custody for three days.

Reader Four: [18] On the third day, Joseph said to them, "Do this and you will live, for I fear God: ¹⁹ If you are honest men, let one of your brothers stay here in prison, while the rest of you go and take grain back for your starving households. ²⁰ But you must bring your youngest brother to me, so that your words may be verified and that you may not die." This they proceeded to do.

²¹ They said to one another, "Surely we are being punished because of our brother. We saw how distressed he was when he pleaded with us for his life, but we would not listen; that's why this distress has come upon us."

²² Reuben replied, "Didn't I tell you not to sin against the boy? But you wouldn't listen! Now we must give an accounting for his blood." ²³ They did not realize that Joseph could understand them, since he was using an interpreter. ²⁴ He turned away from them and began to weep, but then turned back and spoke to them again. He had Simeon taken from them and bound before their eyes.

Genesis 45

Reader Five: ¹ Then Joseph could no longer control himself before all his attendants, and he cried out, "Have everyone leave my presence!" So there was no one with Joseph when he made himself known to his brothers. ² And he wept so loudly that the Egyptians heard him, and Pharaoh's household heard about it.

³ Joseph said to his brothers, "I am Joseph! Is my father still living?" But his brothers were not able to answer him, because they were terrified at his presence.

⁴ Then Joseph said to his brothers, "Come close to me." When they had done so, he said, "I am

your brother Joseph, the one you sold into Egypt! [5] And now, do not be distressed and do not be angry with yourselves for selling me here, because it was to save lives that God sent me ahead of you. [6] For two years now there has been famine in the land, and for the next five years there will not be plowing and reaping. [7] But God sent me ahead of you to preserve for you a remnant on earth and to save your lives by a great deliverance.

[8] "So then, it was not you who sent me here, but God. He made me father to Pharaoh, lord of his entire household and ruler of all Egypt.

Genesis 50
Reader Six: [15] When Joseph's brothers saw that their father was dead, they said, "What if Joseph holds a grudge against us and pays us back for all the wrongs we did to him?" [16] So they sent word to Joseph, saying, "Your father left these instructions before he died: [17] 'This is what you are to say to Joseph: I ask you to forgive your brothers the sins and the wrongs they committed in treating you so badly.' Now please forgive the sins of the servants of the God of your father." When their message came to him, Joseph wept.

[18] His brothers then came and threw themselves down before him. "We are your slaves," they said. [19] But Joseph said to them, "Don't be afraid. Am I in the place of God? [20] You intended to harm me, but God intended it for good to accomplish what is now being done, the saving of many lives. [21] So then, don't be afraid. I will provide for you and your children." And he reassured them and spoke kindly to them.

Genesis 41:56–42:24; 45:1–8; 50:15–21 (NIV)

DISCUSSION QUESTIONS

SELECT FOUR OR FIVE QUESTIONS FROM THE HEAD AND/OR
HEART SECTIONS, OR MAKE UP YOUR OWN

○ Why did Joseph send his brothers away?

○ Why did he hold one of his brothers in prison
while the others went home?

○ Why do you think Joseph's brothers did not
recognize him, even though he recognized
them?

○ Joseph first said that he would keep all the
brothers in prison and only let one go
(42:14–16), then did the opposite (42:18–19).
Why do you think he changed his mind?

○ When Joseph told his brothers who he really
was, they were "terrified" (45:3). Why? Why
were they not overjoyed?

○ Who was ultimately responsible for Joseph's
fate (45:8)? According to Joseph, why was he
sold into slavery (45:5)?

○ Why do you think Joseph "spoke harshly"
(42:7) to his brothers? What would you have
said to them?

○ Did Joseph desire to get even with his brothers?
If not, what did he desire?

○ If you were Joseph, what would you have done

(51)

when your brothers came to you looking for food?

○ Why do you think Joseph wept during these encounters (42:24, 45:2)? What emotion was he feeling?

○ If you'd been one of the ten brothers, how would you have reacted when Joseph suddenly told you who he was?

○ What things do you need to forgive your brothers or sisters? How will you work on reconciliation with them?

○ What things have you done to a brother or sister that may have hurt them? How will you make amends?

CARING FOR ONE ANOTHER

USE THESE QUESTIONS OR MAKE UP YOUR OWN

○ This week, what do you need to apologize for to your brothers or sisters? If you are an only child, how about those closest to you? When will you do so? How can this group pray for you?

○ What will you do this week to forgive things that your brothers or sisters have done to you? How can this group help you to heal from the hurt?

○ How can you become a better brother or sister to your siblings or a better best friend if you are an only child?

This week we found that God can bring reconciliation to families, even when family members have done the most horrible things to one another. In the coming week, be praying for your own family, and for the families in our group, that God will bring about His perfect plan in all our lives. Next week we will consider how God works even in the lives of people who don't have a traditional family.

NOTES

NOTES ON GENESIS 41:56—42:24; 45:1-8; 50:15-21

Read the entire story of Joseph's reconciliation in Genesis 41–50.

42:7 [Joseph] spoke harshly to them. While Joseph's major goal here was to bring healing and reconciliation, he did not minimize the sin that his brothers committed. He recognized that God ordained his entire ordeal, but also held his brothers accountable for their actions. To pretend that someone's sin is insignificant does not bring about healing or reconciliation; the victim also needs to acknowledge the harm done to him in order to forgive it. **From the land of Canaan.** An important progression takes place in this passage, as Joseph gradually forces his brothers to remember and confess their sin. They begin as simple men from Canaan, then become brothers (42:11), then confess that there was another brother who now "is no more" (42:13), then begin to feel remorse and fear for their sin—which they freely confess to one another (42:21). Even then they blamed others rather than themselves (42:22). But gradually we watch them repent of their sin, as first Rueben (42:37) and then Judah (43:8–10) offered their own lives or son's lives in exchange for brother Benjamin, which is the opposite of the way they'd treated Joseph.

42:17 he put them all in custody. Joseph, who has complete power over his brothers, can do anything he desires to them. However, rather than get even, he wants to be reconciled, and his every action shows grace and mercy. It is good for the brothers to experience prison, where Joseph lived for several years, yet Joseph appears to decide that they don't all need to suffer there for very long. It is partly due to mercy, and partly to shrewdness, that Joseph sends most of his brothers home, since it gives them all an opportunity to confront their guilt—and their father—in the process. **for three days.** The story of Joseph has many parallels to that of Christ, including the period of three days in prison, the time the Lord spent in the tomb.

42:18 for I fear God. God's direct hand of guidance is clearly seen throughout Joseph's story (39:2, 39:9, 39:21, etc.), accomplishing His own plan regardless of the wickedness of men. God's plan in Joseph's life includes moving the nation of Israel to Egypt (and from there to the promised land),

and it also includes complete reconciliation and healing within Joseph's family. This point may be very encouraging and helpful to any in the group whose family life is difficult.

42:20 you must bring your youngest brother to me. Joseph sends his brothers away for several reasons. First, he desires that all twelve be united together as a family, getting beyond the fact that the brothers are all sons of four different mothers. Second, he needs to discover whether or not his brothers have really repented of their sin against him, and he chooses to place them in a situation where they will be forced to remember what they have done.

42:24 He had Simeon taken from them and bound. Joseph keeps one of his brothers as a prisoner in order to ensure that the others will return. This also gives Simeon a sense of what Joseph had to endure, and it gives the others a chance to demonstrate their changed hearts by returning, when abandoning Simeon would have been easy.

45:8 it was not you who sent me here, but God. Joseph recognizes that it was God's plan all along that he be sent to Egypt. God chose to train Joseph through his trials to be prepared for the great task he was to eventually fulfill, a task that both saved his family and set the stage for the exodus to the promised land. This is a very important truth for all Christians, that God allows people to do evil against us in order to fulfill His own plan for our lives. God is always in control.

HANG TIME

FAMILY FUNK

ADOPTION: GOD'S CHOSEN FAMILY

EXODUS 1:8-17; 2:1-10

None of us gets to choose the family that we're born into; that is God's choice. Some children are given up by their natural families and are raised by others; this also is God's choice. This is the focus of our study on adoption: that God is in control over our lives, and He chooses what family we are put into. Many kids today are raised by adoptive parents or foster parents; some are raised in a succession of foster homes. These experiences may be traumatic for some and not for others. Your group may have a mixture of young people who have varied experiences with adoptive parents.

We will take a look at the early life of Moses and focus on how God took him away from his family and put him in the home of Pharaoh. While this passage does not explicitly state that God was orchestrating Moses' adoption, we can quickly recognize that truth by realizing that Moses was trained by Pharaoh's family to prepare him for his role in leading the Israelites out of Egypt and into the promised land.

Even if you have no group members who were adopted or raised in foster homes, this study will still be of real value in learning that God is in control of every event in our lives, and He uses our families to prepare us for the plan that He has.

ACTIVITIES

CHOOSE ONE OF THE ACTIVITIES BELOW

○ **Who's this?**
Have each person in the group write down something true about himself that nobody else knows—"I was born on a farm" or "I once ate a grasshopper." Collect the "secrets" and read them aloud, having the group try to guess who wrote each one.

○ **Moses in the Bullrushes**
Break the group into smaller groups, and have each design and build a newspaper boat (or paper airplane, etc.). Have categories, such as most realistic, most creative, longest floating (or farthest flying), and declare winners for each category. (Give a category award to each group.)

ICEBREAKERS

CHOOSE ONE OR TWO OF THESE ICEBREAKERS

○ As a kid, who was your favorite adult friend and why? If you babysit now, work with kids, or know some young children, who is your favorite "customer?"

○ What is the hardest job or chore you've ever done? Did you learn anything new by doing it?

○ Where is the most distant or interesting place that you've gone without your family?

SCRIPTURE READING

READ THE FOLLOWING PASSAGES

Exodus 1

Reader One: [8] Then a new king, who did not know about Joseph, came to power in Egypt. [9] "Look," he said to his people, "the Israelites have become much too numerous for us. [10] Come, we must deal shrewdly with them or they will become even more numerous and, if war breaks out, will join our enemies, fight against us and leave the country."

Reader Two: [11] So they put slave masters over them to oppress them with forced labor, and they built Pithom and Rameses as store cities for Pharaoh. [12] But the more they were oppressed, the more they multiplied and spread; so the Egyptians came to dread the Israelites [13] and worked them ruthlessly. [14] They made their lives bitter with hard labor in brick and mortar and with all kinds of work in the fields; in all their hard labor the Egyptians used them ruthlessly.

Reader Three: [15] The king of Egypt said to the Hebrew midwives, whose names were Shiphrah and Puah, [16] "When you help the Hebrew women in childbirth and observe them on the delivery stool, if it is a boy, kill him; but if it is a girl, let her live." [17] The midwives, however, feared God and did not do what the king of Egypt had told them to do; they let the boys live.

²² Then Pharaoh gave this order to all his people: "Every boy that is born you must throw into the Nile, but let every girl live."

Exodus 2

Reader Four: ¹ Now a man of the house of Levi married a Levite woman, ² and she became pregnant and gave birth to a son. When she saw that he was a fine child, she hid him for three months. ³ But when she could hide him no longer, she got a papyrus basket for him and coated it with tar and pitch. Then she placed the child in it and put it among the reeds along the bank of the Nile. ⁴ His sister stood at a distance to see what would happen to him.

Reader Five: ⁵ Then Pharaoh's daughter went down to the Nile to bathe, and her attendants were walking along the river bank. She saw the basket among the reeds and sent her slave girl to get it. ⁶ She opened it and saw the baby. He was crying, and she felt sorry for him. "This is one of the Hebrew babies," she said.

⁷ Then his sister asked Pharaoh's daughter, "Shall I go and get one of the Hebrew women to nurse the baby for you?"

Reader Six: ⁸ "Yes, go," she answered. And the girl went and got the baby's mother. ⁹ Pharaoh's daughter said to her, "Take this baby and nurse him for me, and I will pay you." So the woman took the baby and nursed him. ¹⁰ When the child grew older, she took him to Pharaoh's daughter and he became her son. She named him Moses, saying, "I drew him out of the water."

Exodus 1:8–17; 2:1–10 (NIV)

DISCUSSION QUESTIONS

SELECT FOUR OR FIVE QUESTIONS FROM THE HEAD AND/OR
HEART SECTIONS, OR MAKE UP YOUR OWN

○ Why does Pharaoh command that all male children must be drowned?

○ Why do the Hebrew midwives refuse to kill babies?

○ What does it cost Moses' family to save his life? What does it cost Moses?

○ What good things does Moses enjoy as a result of being adopted?

○ How can you tell from this passage that God is controlling Moses' fate?

○ Why does God cause Moses to be adopted by Pharaoh? What might have happened if he hadn't been adopted?

○ How do you think Moses felt growing up, knowing that he was not really a son of the people raising him?

○ How do you think Moses felt, knowing that he was actually a member of a slave class of people? How might he have felt conflicted being raised by the people who mistreated his true birth parents?

○ If you were adopted, do you sometimes wonder

61

who your birth family might be? What sort of feelings do you have toward them? Do you feel loved and accepted by your adoptive family?

○ Is God in control of the events in your life, or was Moses just special?

○ What good things can be experienced as a result of being adopted?

CARING FOR ONE ANOTHER

USE THESE QUESTIONS OR MAKE UP YOUR OWN

○ How does knowing that God is in control of your life make you feel? How will it affect your attitude this coming week?

○ What things are you grateful for that you have enjoyed as a result of your family? How can you say thank you for those things?

○ How can you encourage others who have been raised by adoptive or foster families? What lessons from the life of Moses can you use to help them?

NEXT WEEK

This week we discovered that God is completely in control of all events of our lives, right down to hand-picking the family in which we grow up. In the coming week, ask God to bless your parents and family members, thanking Him that He chose to place you in the family that He did. Next week we will talk about some more difficult things that can sometimes happen in families; it will be a hard study, but we will again learn that God has complete control over our lives.

NOTES

NOTES ON EXODUS 1:8-17; 2:1-10

Read all of Exodus 1–3 to get a broader understanding of Moses' upbringing and how it influenced his future ministry.

1:8 Then a new king. Our studies on Joseph ("Sibling Rivalry") have set the background for how the Israelites came to Egypt. When they arrived, they were treated with honor and given the best places in the land to live. One of their own was in the highest position in the land. However, the tables had turned, and the people are despised and treated as slaves. Circumstances for the Israelites seemed horrible, and they probably wondered if God had abandoned them. But God had a larger plan, and He was still completely in control. There are times when our home life can seem that way, too, and it is important that we remember that God is always in control, orchestrating every event in our lives for His own purposes.

1:11 slave masters. The Israelites were an outcast group, the lowest people in the land. They would have been considered as mere property, much as the African-Americans were during our own slave era—people with little worth, and something to be ashamed of. This would put Moses in an odd position as he got older, since he would be raised by the very people who hated his own birth family. Perhaps Moses even felt some sort of conflict himself, wanting to be grateful and to love his adoptive family, but hating the way his own people were oppressed. This conflict becomes apparent in 2:11 and following, as Moses defends a Hebrew by killing an Egyptian who was oppressing him.

1:17 The midwives, however, feared God. The midwives disobeyed the law of Pharaoh because they felt that it violated God's law. God was pleased by this and rewarded them with families of their own (1:21). Today, abortion is the legal alternative to adoption; parents who for any number of reasons feel they can't handle the birth, end the pregnancy with an abortion. It may be worthwhile to touch on this subject here, since people raised by adoption or foster parents may struggle with issues of self-worth. This may prove too controversial a subject, but some young people may need help in understanding this issue; they have heard about the controversy from extreme positions.

2:1–4 Note that the names of Moses' birth family—parents and sister—are not given in this passage. This emphasizes the fact that Moses probably didn't know the identities of his birth family until much later in life, something that most adopted children can relate to.

2:10 Pharaoh's daughter. We learn in Acts 7:22 that Moses was brought up as a prince in Pharaoh's household, receiving the very best education and training available. This helped him in many ways as he led the Israelites out of Egypt, including the fact that he was acquainted with people in power. His education, training, and his previous association with Pharaoh's household gave him the opportunity later to be the spokesman for the Hebrews. His close family connection with Pharaoh himself would have certainly opened the way for him to come before Pharaoh— although it was a different Pharaoh who was in power at the time of the exodus. **he became her son.** Although Moses' family was permitted to keep him for a time, they ultimately had to let him become someone else's son in order to save his life. There was, therefore, no way of keeping him as their own boy; they had to put him up for adoption just to keep him alive. Moses apparently knew that he'd been adopted—note that 3:1 tells us that he knew who "his own people" really were—that is, the Hebrews, not the Egyptians. But this was all part of God's plan for Moses' life; He had a job for Moses to do, and Moses had to be adopted by a different family to fulfill that purpose. It may be helpful to those in the group who were foster children or adopted to know that God ordains the family we grow up in for a specific purpose. Of course, the same applies to those of us who grew up in our true birth families: God uses our families to prepare us to serve Him.

HANG TIME

FAMILY FUNK

6 ABUSE

This study is going to be the most painful one in this book, since it deals with rape and sexual abuse. It is deliberate that we have saved it until now: our previous studies have shown us clearly that God controls all events in our lives, and our next study will show us what a perfect Father He is.

Still the questions remain: what possible good could God intend from such a horrible sin? Why did He allow this to happen in the first place? The difficult truth of life is that God does allow people to do terrible things to one another, and sometimes we cannot easily find a happy conclusion. Consider, for example, Cain murdering his own brother Abel. God allowed Cain to kill Abel, and He did not miraculously raise Abel again from the dead.

The story of Ammon and his lust for Tamar follows immediately after David's sin with Bathsheba and his murder of her husband, Uriah. See 2 Samuel 11, and 12:11-12 for more information. This is an example of how a person's sin will often be carried on by his children, carrying abuse into subsequent generations.

Christians are sometimes called upon to cling to the belief that God is in control at all times, even when it seems as though He is absent. Sometimes we can look back later and see how He used it for His purposes; sometimes we cannot. Certainly in the case of sexual abuse it is difficult to find any good things that may come of it. The focus of this study is on the reality of terrible sin in the lives of human beings, even innocent humans who have done nothing to deserve such treatment. It is also on the responsibility of all humans to act in obedience to God, including those who are tempted to sin and those who are aware of crimes against children.

If any in your group are victims of abuse in their families, this study will be difficult. It may also bring to light things that have happened in their homes, perhaps that are still happening. If this is the case, remember that a youth group leader is legally required to report such things to the authorities. It is not an option. All the same, this study can become a very important step in healing for those who have suffered from abuse, and in repentance for those who may have been tempted.

Note: The opening activities and icebreaker questions this week are deliberately unrelated to the story.

ACTIVITIES

CHOOSE ONE OF THE ACTIVITIES BELOW

○ **Sardines**
Sardines is the opposite of hide and seek. One person is "it," but instead of seeking, "it" hides and the rest of the group try to find "it." When a person finds the one who is "it," he scrunches in to hide with him. The last person to find the group becomes "it."

○ **Name that Flavor**
Set out a series of bowls of ice cream, or glasses of soda, or some other flavored food. Each person has a sheet of paper, and must guess (from just one taste) what each flavor is. If necessary, have people blindfolded when tasting. Have some easy ones, like chocolate ice cream, and some hard ones, like cinnamon apple ice cream.

○ Who is your favorite movie star, and why?

○ What flavor of ice cream do you most often order? Do you prefer a cone or a dish?

○ If you could be king or queen for a day, what would you do?

SCRIPTURE READING

READ THE FOLLOWING PASSAGES

Read the following passage from 2 Samuel 13. [Note: Due to the sensitive nature of the content, you may prefer to have just one person read, or maybe do it yourself.]

Reader One: ¹ In the course of time, Amnon son of David fell in love with Tamar, the beautiful sister of Absalom son of David. ² Amnon became frustrated to the point of illness on account of his sister Tamar, for she was a virgin, and it seemed impossible for him to do anything to her.

³ Now Amnon had a friend named Jonadab son of Shimeah, David's brother. Jonadab was a very shrewd man. ⁴ He asked Amnon, "Why do you, the king's son, look so haggard morning after morning? Won't you tell me?"

Amnon said to him, "I'm in love with Tamar, my brother Absalom's sister."

[5] "Go to bed and pretend to be ill," Jonadab said. "When your father comes to see you, say to him, 'I would like my sister Tamar to come and give me something to eat. Let her prepare the food in my sight so I may watch her and then eat it from her hand.' "

Reader Two: [6] So Amnon lay down and pretended to be ill. When the king came to see him, Amnon said to him, "I would like my sister Tamar to come and make some special bread in my sight, so I may eat from her hand."

[7] David sent word to Tamar at the palace: "Go to the house of your brother Amnon and prepare some food for him." [8] So Tamar went to the house of her brother Amnon, who was lying down. She took some dough, kneaded it, made the bread in his sight and baked it. [9] Then she took the pan and served him the bread, but he refused to eat.

"Send everyone out of here," Amnon said. So everyone left him. [10] Then Amnon said to Tamar, "Bring the food here into my bedroom so I may eat from your hand." And Tamar took the bread she had prepared and brought it to her brother Amnon in his bedroom. [11] But when she took it to him to eat, he grabbed her and said, "Come to bed with me, my sister."

Reader Three: [12] "Don't, my brother!" she said to him. "Don't force me. Such a thing should not be done in Israel! Don't do this wicked thing. [13] What about me? Where could I get rid of my disgrace? And what about you? You would be like one of the wicked fools in Israel. Please speak to the king; he will not keep me from being married to you."

¹⁴ But he refused to listen to her, and since he was stronger than she, he raped her.

¹⁵ Then Amnon hated her with intense hatred. In fact, he hated her more than he had loved her. Amnon said to her, "Get up and get out!"

¹⁶ "No!" she said to him. "Sending me away would be a greater wrong than what you have already done to me." But he refused to listen to her. ¹⁷ He called his personal servant and said, "Get this woman out of here and bolt the door after her." ¹⁸ So his servant put her out and bolted the door after her. She was wearing a richly ornamented robe, for this was the kind of garment the virgin daughters of the king wore. ¹⁹ Tamar put ashes on her head and tore the ornamented robe she was wearing. She put her hand on her head and went away, weeping aloud as she went.

Reader Four: ²⁰ Her brother Absalom said to her, "Has that Amnon, your brother, been with you? Be quiet now, my sister; he is your brother. Don't take this thing to heart." And Tamar lived in her brother Absalom's house, a desolate woman.

²¹ When King David heard all this, he was furious. ²² Absalom never said a word to Amnon, either good or bad; he hated Amnon because he had disgraced his sister Tamar.

Reader Five: ²³ Two years later, when Absalom's sheepshearers were at Baal Hazor near the border of Ephraim, he invited all the king's sons to come there.

²⁸ Absalom ordered his men, "Listen! When Amnon is in high spirits from drinking wine and I say to you, 'Strike Amnon down,' then kill

him. Don't be afraid. Have not I given you this order? Be strong and brave." ²⁹ So Absalom's men did to Amnon what Absalom had ordered. Then all the king's sons got up, mounted their mules and fled.

2 Samuel 13:1–23,28–29 (NIV)

DISCUSSION QUESTIONS

SELECT FOUR OR FIVE QUESTIONS FROM THE HEAD AND/OR HEART SECTIONS, OR MAKE UP YOUR OWN

○ Why does Amnon need to go to such lengths to attack Tamar?

○ Tamar never suspects Amnon's true motives until it is too late. What does this suggest about her character?

○ What motivates Amnon to attack his sister?

○ Why does Amnon suddenly hate Tamar after attacking her? Why does he throw her out?

○ What are the results of this crime in Tamar's life? In the entire family?

○ Why does Absalom tell his sister, "Be quiet now" (V. 20)? What should he have done instead?

○ Why do you think Amnon grew ill with longing for Tamar? Do you think he loved her?

○ Tamar let Absalom know what happened, and he did nothing. How do you think Tamar felt?

○ Amnon may have thought he really loved his sister initially. How should he have handled his longing properly?

○ What does Tamar mean in verse 16, "Sending me away would be a greater wrong than what you have already done to me"? How does Amnon's hatred and rejection make Tamar's injury even worse?

○ If you had been Absalom, what would you have done? If you had been David? If you had been Tamar?

CARING FOR ONE ANOTHER

USE THESE QUESTIONS OR MAKE UP YOUR OWN

○ If you or someone you know is the victim of abuse, speak with a mature adult privately.

○ Spend time in silent prayer:

○ If you have suffered abuse, tell God all about it. Turn it over to Him and ask Him to make things whole again. Speak to a mature adult in private.

○ If you struggle with the temptations that Amnon faced, ask God to lead you away from temptation and guide you to godliness. Speak to a mature adult in private.

○ How can the group help any who are tempted toward mistreating others?

○ How can the group help those who have been mistreated like this?

NEXT WEEK

This week we have addressed a very painful topic, looking at a family that was torn apart by sexual abuse. In the coming week, if you have suffered similar abuse, pray that God will give you the courage to talk about it with someone who can help. Next week we will conclude this study with the good news that God is not like human fathers, and that He is eager to be the perfect Father to all of His children.

NOTES

NOTES ON 2 SAMUEL 13:1-23,28-29

13:1 sister of Absalom. David has what we would today call a blended family; Amnon and Tamar have different mothers but the same father. Amnon is David's oldest, the heir to the throne.

13:2 Amnon became frustrated. Amnon may have been truly in love with his sister, simply infatuated, or merely lustful. Regardless, she is his sister so his attentions are misplaced.

13:5 Jonadab shares guilt in this sin. To know of such an abusive situation and not to intervene is the same as enabling it to continue; how much more, then, to help the abuser plan the sin.

13:7 David sent word to Tamar. Situations like this may not be easily apparent to outsiders, or even to other family members. David does not seem to suspect any evil intentions in his son's request.

13:8-10 Tamar willingly serves her brother, trusting him to the very moment when he grabs her. She never suspects his evil intentions, trusting him completely since he is her brother. This is one of the most devastating aspects of such abuse, since it takes advantage of a loving trust which should be protected, not violated.

13:15 Amnon hated her. With his lust satisfied, Amnon's "love" turns to hatred. He cannot stand to have her near him, because it reminds him of his own sin. His disgust is really at himself, but (like many abusers) he takes it out on her, having a servant throw her out and bolt the door behind her.

13:16 a greater wrong than what you have already done. Tamar's primary fear is that she will now be unsuitable as a wife for any other man. Victims of such abuse often feel that they are somehow responsible for what has happened, and that they are dirty and unfit to ever love someone. Amnon reinforces this false reaction by throwing her out of his house as though she were the guilty person. Abuse victims may struggle most of their lives with a deep sense of guilt and shame, even though they were the innocent victims.

13:20 Be quiet now. Absalom and David demonstrate wrong responses to this situation. Absalom determines to take his own revenge where he has no authority, and David—who is the king and therefore does have authority—does nothing. Absalom's response leads to further violence and destruction within the home; David's lack of response leaves the abuser free to harm others.

FAMILY FUNK

7 THE PERFECT FATHER

LUKE 15:11-32

Our final study sums up the large truth that we have been considering in all of the previous studies: that God is in control of all events in our lives, and that He is the perfect Father. This study focuses on Jesus' parable known as "The Prodigal Son," which some say should really be called "The Gracious Father."

In this parable, the Lord contrasts our treatment of God (represented by the two sons) with the gracious, compassionate love of God toward us. Thus, we can learn as much about ourselves as we can about God as we read the story.

In our previous studies, we have dealt with many types of hardship and tension that can develop in human families. In this study, we will see that God is the ultimate Father of all His children. As the Father, He is in control of all that we experience, and He is always eager to embrace us whether we have been "prodigal" or "stay-at home" children.

The focus of this study is not meant to speak badly of human fathers, but rather to bring the good news that there is a perfect Father who is guiding His children with love and compassion. It is a very encouraging message, regardless of what our family lives are like, to learn that the final authority in our homes is God Himself.

ACTIVITIES

CHOOSE ONE OF THE ACTIVITIES BELOW

○ **Prodigal Shoes**
Have everyone remove their shoes, piling them all in the middle of the room. Turn off the lights and call "go," having everyone scramble to recover his own footwear.

○ **Milk the Cow**
Fill several latex gloves with water, tie them shut, and suspend them from a horizontal broom handle with a tiny hole in the bottom of one or all fingers of each glove. Have a timed relay race: blow a whistle; one person from each team milks his team's glove for 10 seconds; then blow the whistle for the next person. First empty glove wins.

ICEBREAKERS

CHOOSE ONE OR TWO OF THESE ICEBREAKERS

○ What is the strangest thing you've ever eaten?

○ Describe a perfect party or celebration. Who would be there? What would you eat? What entertainment would you have?

○ If you were given a million dollars tomorrow, what would you do?

Reader One: [11] "A man had two sons. [12] The younger of them said to his father, 'Father, give me the share of the estate I have coming to me.' So he distributed the assets to them. [13] Not many days later, the younger son gathered together all he had and traveled to a distant country, where he squandered his estate in foolish living. [14] After he had spent everything, a severe famine struck that country, and he had nothing. [15] Then he went to work for one of the citizens of that country, who sent him into his fields to feed pigs. [16] He longed to eat his fill from the carob pods the pigs were eating, and no one would give him any. [17] But when he came to his senses, he said, 'How many of my father's hired hands have more than enough food, and here I am dying of hunger! [18] I'll get up, go to my father, and say to him, "Father, I have sinned against heaven and in your sight. [19] I'm no longer worthy to be called your son. Make me like one of your hired hands."' [20] So he got up and went to his father. But while the son was still a long way off, his father saw him and was filled with compassion. He ran, threw his arms around his neck, and kissed him. [21] The son said to him, 'Father, I have sinned against heaven and in your sight. I'm no longer worthy to be called your son.'

Reader Two: [22] "But the father told his slaves, 'Quick! Bring out the best robe and put it on him; put a ring on his finger and sandals on his feet. 23 Then bring the fattened calf and slaughter it, and let's celebrate with a feast, 24 because this son of mine was dead and is alive again; he was lost and is found!' So they began to celebrate.

25 "Now his older son was in the field; as he came near the house, he heard music and dancing. 26 So he summoned one of the servants and asked what these things meant. 27 'Your brother is here,' he told him, 'and your father has slaughtered the fattened calf because he has him back safe and sound.'

Reader Three: 28 "Then he became angry and didn't want to go in. So his father came out and pleaded with him. 29 But he replied to his father, 'Look, I have been slaving many years for you, and I have never disobeyed your orders; yet you never gave me a young goat so I could celebrate with my friends. 30 But when this son of yours came, who has devoured your assets with prostitutes, you slaughtered the fattened calf for him.'

31 " 'Son,' he said to him, 'you are always with me, and everything I have is yours. 32 But we had to celebrate and rejoice, because this brother of yours was dead and is alive again; he was lost and is found.' "

Luke 15:11–32

DISCUSSION QUESTIONS

O Why do you think the younger son wanted his inheritance early? Why did he travel "to a distant country" (v. 13)?

O What does it mean that the young man "came to his senses" (v. 17)? Why did it take him so long to decide to go home?

O Why does the young man conclude that he is "no longer worthy" to be called his father's son (v. 19)? What sins has he committed (v. 18)?

O Why does the father run out to meet his son "while the son was still a long way off" (v. 20)? What would you have expected him to do?

O Why does the father give his son new clothes and a party? Why doesn't he punish him instead?

O Why is the older brother angry?

O How do you think the young man felt when he was living at home, son of a wealthy man with many servants? How do you think he felt while feeding pigs?

O What would it have been like for him to return home and become just a hired servant?

○ If you'd been the young man, how would you have reacted to having your father run out to greet you this way (v. 20)?

○ If you'd been the father, how would you have reacted when the son returned? When the older son got angry?

○ Which son are you more like, the older or the younger? Why?

CARING FOR ONE ANOTHER

USE THESE QUESTIONS OR MAKE UP YOUR OWN

○ Are you living in the love of God, who is the only perfect Father? Or are you like the younger son, running away from the Father's love and riches?

○ Do you tend to look toward humans for unconditional love and acceptance? How will you start turning to God to be your Father this coming week?

○ Do you sometimes treat others with resentment, the way the older brother did? Where do you have need to repent of this attitude this week?

NOTES ON LUKE 15:11-32

15:12 the share of the estate. This was actually a very rude request; the sons would normally not receive their inheritance until after the father had died. It suggests that the son does not care much about his father, but is only interested in his wealth. In contrast, however, the father's attitudes and actions indicate that he cares little about his wealth and everything about his two sons.

15:13 distant country. The young man's focus is on worldly pursuits—he wants to see the world and live life to its fullest. The distant country may also suggest his determination to get as far away as possible from home and family, and would have allowed him to do as he pleased without his father watching.

15:15 feed pigs. This work is certainly lowly in any culture, but for a Jew it would have been considered the ultimate disgrace. Pigs were unclean animals according to Old Testament law (Lev. 11:7), and this young man has completely disgraced and defiled himself by the time he eats with them.

15:17 came to his senses. This appears to be the point of repentance for the young man, when he finally decides to humble himself and return to his father. He finally harbors no illusions as to his own sin; he is right when he declares that he is "no longer worthy" to be called a son. That is the very point of this parable: neither son is worthy, yet the father delights in loving them anyway.

15:20 a long way off. The father spots his son long before he arrives home, implying that he'd been watching and waiting for him all along. Jesus is emphasizing how deeply the Father loves His children, and how He longs for us to be in daily communion with Him. The father's delight pours out in eager welcome, kisses, hugs, costly gifts, and a big celebration.

15:22 robe...ring...sandals. The son returns barefoot and destitute, but he is clothed with honor. The "best robe" and ring indicate that he is an honored guest, perhaps even one who has authority over the servants (signet rings, for example, were signs of authority).

15:28 he became angry. The older son is actually no better than his brother; his refusal to join the party is just as rude as his brother's request for his inheritance. His focus seems to be on getting rewarded for his faithful service. This is not a fitting attitude for a son; it makes him no better than one of the hired servants. Jesus is emphasizing that, since God is our Father, we should rejoice in His love and compassion and availability to us, not in the rewards and pleasures He can give us.

15:29 slaving. Here again, the older son shows his true focus: he has been faithful to the father, not out of love or gratitude, but out of a mercenary spirit, expecting reward. This has led to his bitter cynicism, since such service is truly a form of slavery. Ironically, the one who now appreciates this distinction is the younger son.

15:30–32 this son of yours ... this brother of yours. The older brother's anger and self-righteousness cause him to reject his own brother, but the father gently corrects him.